BRAIN ACADEMY

Steph King
and
Richard Cooper

MATHS CHALLENGES

MISSION FILE 5
For more able mathematicians in Year 6

Rising Stars UK Ltd, 7 Hatchers Mews, Bermondsey Street, London, SE1 3GS

www.risingstars-uk.com

Published in association with  National Association for Able Children in Education

Published 2014
Text, design and layout © Rising Stars UK Ltd. 2014

Authors: Steph King and Richard Cooper
Series Consultant: Cherri Moseley
Text design and typesetting: Steve Evans Design and Illustration
Cover design: Lon Chan, Words & Pictures Ltd, London
Publisher: Fiona Lazenby
Editorial: Lynette Woodward and Sparks Publishing Services, Ltd
Illustrations: Bill Greenhead (characters) and Steve Evans Design and Illustration

British Library Cataloguing in Publication Data.
A CIP record for this book is available from the British Library.

ISBN: 978-1-78339-233-9

Printed by Newnorth Print, Ltd. Bedford.

Pages 44–45, TASC: Thinking Actively in a Social Context © Belle Wallace 2004

Contents

Welcome to Brain Academy

Da Vinci

The master and founder of Brain Academy. Da Vinci has recently upgraded himself to 'tablet' form. He communicates via his touch screen but doesn't like being prodded and poked by Huxley. Da Vinci is dedicated to eradicating boring maths lessons and solving exciting mathematical problems around the world.

Huxley

Hux is DV's right-hand man. If he can't fix it, no-one can. Huxley carries a 'man-bag' which DV conveniently fits into. Always one for a joke or three, Huxley is the chap who keeps things moving in the right direction. Hopefully, forwards of course.

Rosa

Rosa Spudds is the Brain Academy gardening guru. There is nothing about gardening or 'growing your own' that Rosa doesn't know about. An expert in all fields. (And meadows, hedges, ponds, marshes and farms in general).

Hailey

Hailey Komet gained a PhD in Astrophysics at Oxford. She knows more about wormholes, black holes and any other holes one finds in the depths of the Universe than anyone else on our Planet. Hailey is convinced time travel is possible after the disappearance of the previous team ...

Evan

Evan Elpus is a young inventor from the Welsh Valleys. Da Vinci saw his potential after watching his on-line inventing tutorials, 'Elpus 'Elps You'. Followed everywhere by his Welsh Terrier Dylan, Evan is always up for a challenge. 'Tidy!' as he might say.

Omar

Omar Gosh is the world quiz champion after winning a global edition of 'Faster-mind'. He scored 100% and won on the last question. He knew how tall Mount Everest is ... in centimetres (884,800 cm). As a result, Omar's bank of useful (and useless) knowledge knows no heights.

Gammon

Gammon is the grandson of Ham, the Astro-chimp who flew into space back in 1961. Ham was trained by NASA to pilot a rocket. Gammon has inherited his grandfather's intelligence and has also developed the power of speech. However, this can sometimes be a little awkward due to his, let's say, 'choice of words'. He lives with Hailey Komet whom he 'adopted' earlier.

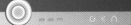

Mason

Mason Stones is a brilliant architect and master of materials, design and space. He can make any building, anywhere. His constructions are built to survive the elements so hurricanes, tsunamis, volcanoes and earthquakes hold no fear for their occupants. That's his theory anyway – he's still drawing up the plans.

Babs

Ms Barbara 'Babs' Babbage is a distant cousin to Charles Babbage, the inventor of the first computer. Ms Babbage has her own micro-chip like mind which is faster than the zippiest broadband in her home county of Devon. Babs has an accent thicker than clotted cream and a heart as warm as tea.

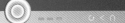

Echo

Once the hippest chick around, these days **Echonia Plant** (**Echo** to her BA friends!) works at Brain Academy part-time when she's not standing as a Green Party MEP. She knows all there is to know about how HQ runs, so she organises and manages communications. She still heads out into the field for the occasional mission when a nature-loving eco-warrior is needed though!

WPC Gallop and PC Trott

WPC Gallop and PC Trott are fearless police officers who lend a helping hand to the Brain Academy team when criminals are on the loose. Their investigative skills are unparalleled.
They do more than just plod about, you know!

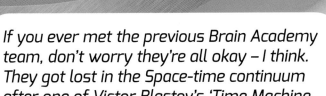

If you ever met the previous Brain Academy team, don't worry they're all okay – I think. They got lost in the Space-time continuum after one of Victor Blastov's 'Time Machine experiments' went wrong. It's just a matter of time before they get back I suppose …

Working with Brain Academy

This tells you where and when each mission takes place. Read the introduction to find out what the problem is and what help the Brain Academy agents need from you.

Start with the Training Mission (TM). This will get you ready for the Main Mission. You will need to use your maths and reasoning skills and explain your thinking.

You will need to find information to help you solve the problems in tables, charts, graphs, and so on. Remember to look carefully!

MISSION 5.5 Alien Algebra

TIME: To look for intelligent life
PLACE: A galaxy, far, far away ...

Babs's wooden computer has churned out some strange algebraic equations and sequences that have been picked up by the Brain Academy Super Computer, which is looking for intelligent life in space.

What was it that the great science fiction writer Arthur C. Clarke said about aliens?

'Sometimes I think we're alone in the Universe and sometimes I think we're not. In either case the idea is quite staggering.'

TM

Find the values of the shapes in each of the equations below.

1) $\blacklozenge \times \dfrac{2}{3} = 18 \div 36$

2) $720 \div$ prime factor of $720 = \dfrac{2}{\blacksquare} \times 50$

3) $0.875 + \blacktriangle = \dfrac{3}{8} \times$

4) In equation 3, if $\blacktriangle$ is a number less than 6, what is the highest possible whole number value of the trapezium?

Gosh, I wonder what this is all about!

16

Now you've met the team, you are ready for your mission briefing!

MM

Find the values of each of the letters in the grid. Each is a whole number.

1) $ab = 36$

2) $\frac{w}{5} = c$

3) $2c + a = 21$

4) $21 + b = v^2$

5) $3v - 2d = 9$

6) $10y - w = 40$

7) $\frac{bx}{2} = w$

a	b	c	d
v	w	x	y

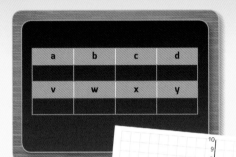

In the Main Mission (MM) you may need to use your answers from the Training Mission to help you. Read the questions carefully and think logically. What information do you have? What do you need to know? Can you use any patterns or rules to help you?

DV FILES

Huxley remembers that a radio signal sequence from 1977 is still the first and best potential evidence of communication with extraterrestrials.

It also remains one of the biggest mysteries in science. But he's not sure if there is any connection to the printouts from Bab's computer ...

Babs is sure that this is a problem about reflection, but she is not sure if she should reflect the coordinates in the x or y axis.

1) Help the team to find a three-letter code word. Write down any new coordinates.

Now I know the connection! You might want to find out a bit more about the sequence Jerry Ehman found in 1977!

Huxley's Helpline

You will need to make a decision about other coordinates that should be joined with lines.

17

If you're brave enough, try a really tricky challenge from Da Vinci in the DV Files. You'll need to use different problem-solving strategies. It might help to talk to a partner or share ideas in a group.

If you get stuck, call Huxley's Helpline for a hint. There are more Mission Strategies to help you on pages 46 and 47, but have a go yourself first! Remember, Brain Academy agents never give up!

Ready for your first mission? Let's go!

TIME: To get out the Welsh phrase book
PLACE: The green, green grass of Evan's home

Gammon is test piloting a new flying car invented by Evan. He is visiting different places around Wales: a real 'fly-drive'. However, the sat-nav has gone wrong and he has trouble navigating ...

This flying car means navigating the Welsh mountains is easy-ee, eeh!

Except you're going round a few of them more than once, Gammon ...

TM

Gammon will start his journey at Wrexham.

1) Use the scale of this map to help you find the actual distances in kilometres for each stage of Gammon's journey.

2) What is the distance of the total journey?

3) The new flying car travels at a top speed of **54 km per hour**. How long will it take to fly from Aberystwyth to Bangor?

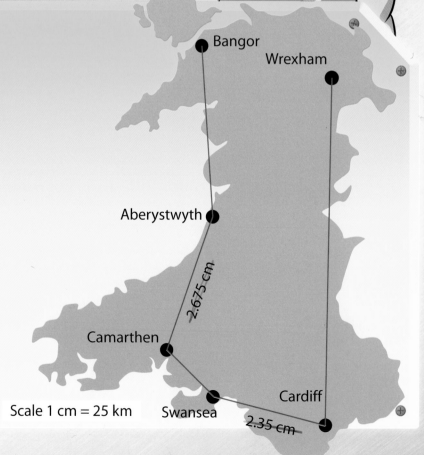

Bangor
Wrexham
Aberystwyth
2.675 cm
Camarthen
Cardiff
Scale 1 cm = 25 km
Swansea
2.35 cm

At the next junction, make a U-turn ...

Gammon starts the first stage of his journey to Cardiff. He is having a grand old time until the sat-nav starts monkeying around!

Gammon is flying in the direction of the red arrow.

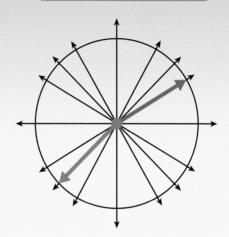

1) How many degrees **anti-clockwise** must he turn to fly in the direction of the **blue** arrow?

2) Things get worse as the sat-nav then tells him to turn through another 285° **clockwise**. Describe his new direction as a turn from the original **red** arrow.

3) He still has $\frac{3}{12}$ of the distance to go to reach Cardiff. How far has he flown so far?

_____ km

4) What distance does he still need to travel to complete the whole trip?

DV FILES

After a further 30 minutes of flying and changing directions, Evan prints out a copy of Gammon's route.

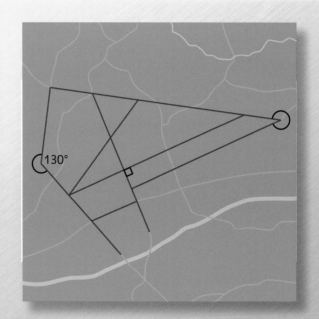

130°

1) Without using a protractor, find the size of all the other internal angles.

2) Now find the size of the two marked external angles.

Oh, only the sizes of two angles have been shown. I need to know all angles if I have any chance of getting Gammon going in the right direction again!

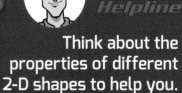

Huxley's Helpline

Think about the properties of different 2-D shapes to help you.

TIME: To be beside the seaside
PLACE: Beside the sea!

The Sea-View Hotel will rapidly become The Beach-View as it sits perilously on top of an eroded cliff. The team has been given the task of moving it to a safer place.

Mason my good fellow. Are your engineering skills up to the challenge?

I could move a mountain if you gave me a long enough pole to use as a lever!

The Sea-View Hotel is owned by Mr and Mrs Riddles. They both love puzzles and have numbered the rooms on each floor in quite a strange way.

1st floor	401	409		421		433
2nd floor	1		4	19		76
3rd floor	-37	-23.5		3.5		
4th floor	343	216		64		8

1) Find the connection between numbers on each floor and fill in the missing door numbers. Check to see if there are any linear sequences.

2) Find some different possibilities for the missing door numbers on the **fifth** floor. Try to be creative!

5th floor	$\frac{19}{8}$		2.375		237.5 %	57 ÷ 24

MM

The team need the help of a construction company to set up cranes and winches to move the hotel. It will be a mammoth task!

1) Write the current coordinates of the hotel.

2) The hotel is moved so that coordinate **c** is at the new position (**−3**, **4**). Describe this translation.

3) Write the new coordinates of **a**, **b** and **d**.

4) The perimeter of the hotel is 456.4 metres. What is the actual length of the wall from **b** to **d**?

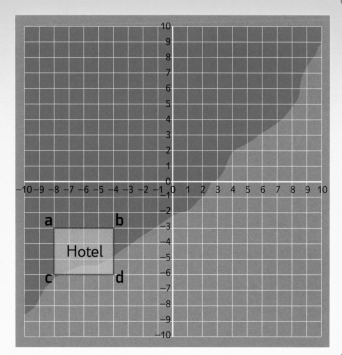

DV FILES

The team must help Mr and Mrs Riddles by re-arranging the masses into different rooms on the ground floor of the hotel so it doesn't topple again.

They must make sure that the mean mass is the same in each row, column and diagonal so that everything balances!

425.7 kg	141.9 kg	47.3 kg
94.6 kg	378.4 kg	283.8 kg
236.5 kg	189.2 kg	331.1 kg

Wow, that was close! The Riddles nearly had the largest outdoor pool ever!

Huxley's Helpline

You may find it useful to write each mass on different pieces of paper so you can move them around the grid.

5.3 App-alling App!

TIME: *Not now, I'm playing* **Dappy-Nerd**
PLACE: *In a virtual world*

A mobile phone app has brain-washed millions of kids around the world. *Dappy-Nerd* has taken over and needs stopping before everyone becomes unable to do their homework.

This pesky app is giving us, err ... 'electronic devices' a bad name.

You've haven't downloaded it have you, Sir?!!

TM

Dappy-Nerd

Top 5 players

	Score
Dymm	9,473,210
Whitt	9,064,595
Nelli	8,909,007
14MDaft	8,395,063
Dizzi	7,884,991

1) Write the value of the digit '9' in each of the scores.

2) How many more points does Dymm need to score to reach a total of 10 million?

3) The player in **sixth** position needs to score the following points in the next few games to equal Dizzi's score.

8500
20,019
134,006

What is their current score?

MM

The problem is worse than they thought. Babs prints out a graph to show the rest of the team.

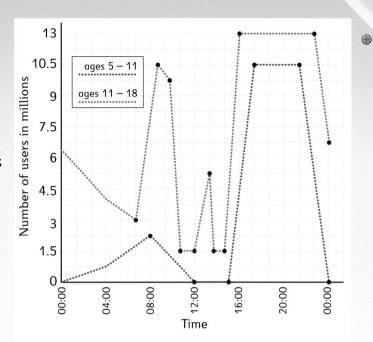

1) Why do you think the numbers of users shown by the blue and red lines are so different at midnight, 8 a.m. and between 12 p.m. and 2 p.m.?

2) What is the difference between the numbers of users at 8 a.m.?
_____**million**

3) What is the greatest number of users in total playing on the App at the same time?

4) For how many hours is this total the same?

And this is only in this country. Just imagine what it is like in the rest of the world!

DV FILES

The team have designed an ingenious upgrade to remove all of *Dappy-Nerd's* brainwashing powers.

But first, the coloured buttons must be pressed in the correct sequence and a code number must be entered into the bottom pink square. This will activate the download.

1) Order the numbers on the buttons from smallest to largest to find the sequence.

2) The code number is the mean of all the other buttons. What is it? Give your answer to the nearest thousandth.

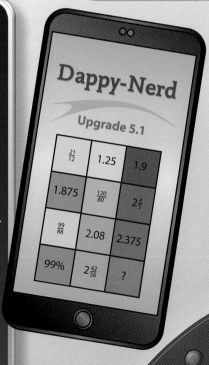

Dappy-Nerd

Upgrade 5.1

$\frac{21}{12}$	1.25	1.9
1.875	$\frac{120}{80}$	$2\frac{4}{5}$
$\frac{99}{88}$	2.08	2.375
99%	$2\frac{42}{56}$	?

Huxley's Helpline

The mean is also known as the average.

5.4 Ocean Deep, Mountain High ...

TIME: *For a deep conversation*
PLACE: *As low as it gets*

Hailey is analysing sea-mud and silt brought up by Gammon from a trip down to the deepest place on earth, the Mariana Trench. He successfully piloted a mini-sub built by Evan.

At least you couldn't get lost on the way up!

Cheeky ee-ee-ee-!

Mariana Trench Fact File

- The Mariana Trench is a crescent-shaped scar in the Earth's crust that measures more than 1500 miles long and 43 miles wide, on average.

- The distance between the surface of the ocean and the trench's deepest point, the Challenger Deep, is nearly 7 miles. If Mount Everest were dropped into the Mariana Trench, its peak would still be more than a mile underwater!

Hailey has been finding out more about the Mariana Trench.

1) Convert all measurements in miles to kilometres.

2) Mount Everest is 8848 metres high. Using 7 miles as the depth of Challenger Deep, find out how far the peak of Mount Everest will be underwater.

———— **metres**

MM

Hailey gets to work analysing the samples of mud and silt. There are nine of these trays in a large box.

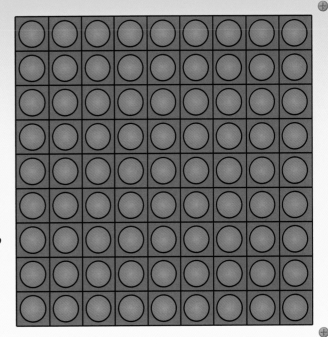

1) So far she has analysed $\frac{2}{9}$ of each tray. What fraction is this of the whole box?

2) Hailey analyses a further $\frac{8}{27}$ of the box. What fraction of the box has now been analysed?

3) How many samples are still left to analyse?

4) Next she analyses $\frac{1}{3}$ of $\frac{7}{9}$ of a tray. Re-write this calculation using division. What fraction of the tray is this?

DV FILES

Hailey puts all the information into the computer and waits for the results ...

The silt and mud are full of minerals that will be of great interest to cosmetic companies for face masks and other treatments for the skin.

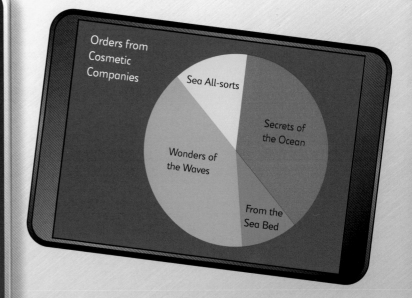

1) Find the percentage of orders from each company.

2) There were 326,400 orders in total. How many more orders did *Wonders of the Waves* make than *Secrets of the Ocean*?

3) A fifth company places another 81,600 orders. What percentage of the total orders does *From the Sea Bed* represent now?

Huxley's Helpline

Remember to use a protractor to help you.

5.5 Alien Algebra

TIME: To look for intelligent life
PLACE: A galaxy, far, far away ...

Babs's wooden computer has churned out some strange algebraic equations and sequences that have been picked up by the Brain Academy Super Computer, which is looking for intelligent life in space.

> What was it that the great science fiction writer Arthur C. Clarke said about aliens?

> 'Sometimes I think we're alone in the Universe and sometimes I think we're not. In either case the idea is quite staggering.'

TM

Find the values of the shapes in each of the equations below.

1) $\diamond \times \dfrac{2}{3} = 18 \div 36$

2) $720 \div \text{prime factor of } 720 = \dfrac{2}{\blacksquare} \times 50$

3) $0.875 + \blacktriangle = \dfrac{3}{8} \times \text{▱}$

4) In equation 3, if ▲ is a number less than 6, what is the highest possible whole number value of ▱?

> Gosh, I wonder what this is all about!

MM

Find the values of each of the letters in the grid. Each is a whole number.

1) $ab = 36$

2) $\dfrac{w}{5} = c$

3) $2c + a = 21$

4) $21 + b = v^2$

5) $3v - 2d = 9$

6) $10y - w = 40$

7) $\dfrac{bx}{2} = w$

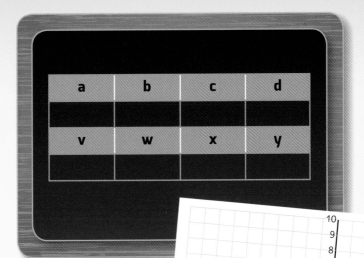

a	b	c	d
v	w	x	y

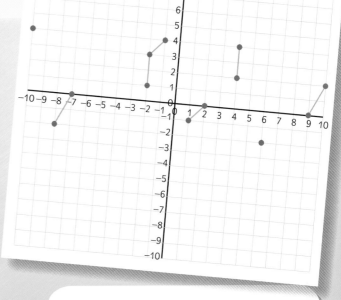

DV FILES

Huxley remembers that a radio signal sequence from 1977 is still the first and best potential evidence of communication with extraterrestrials.

It also remains one of the biggest mysteries in science. But he's not sure if there is any connection to the printouts from Bab's computer ...

Babs is sure that this is a problem about reflection, but she is not sure if she should reflect the coordinates in the x or y axis.

1) Help the team to find a three-letter code word. Write down any new coordinates.

Now I know the connection! You might want to find out a bit more about the sequence Jerry Ehman found in 1977!

Huxley's Helpline

You will need to make a decision about other coordinates that should be joined with lines.

TIME: For the London Marathon
PLACE: London, silly! Keep up please

Hailey and Gammon are running the London Marathon together. Gammon is a little worried because he's not as good on two legs as he is on four.

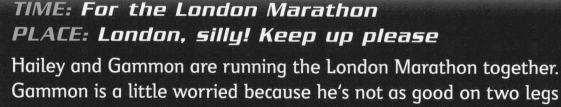

Don't worry Gammon, just do your best.

Am I allowed to swing my way round on the lampposts? Ah-Ah!

Hailey and Gammon will start at 10 a.m. from the green position for celebrities and other runners who are good for their age.

1) The London Marathon is **26.2 miles**. How far is this in kilometres using the conversion 8 km ≈ 5 miles?

2) Poor Gammon is finding it rather difficult to keep up with Hailey. For every $\frac{3}{5}$ mile Hailey runs, Gammon only runs $\frac{3}{8}$ mile. How far behind is he by the time Hailey reaches Canary Wharf (16 miles)?

Hailey works out that she is running a mile in an average of 8 mins 15 secs.

REAL TIME PACE GUIDE

Mile	Elite Women	3:30 Pace	4:30 Pace	5:00 Pace	6:00 Pace	Mile	Elite Women	3:30 Pace	4:30 Pace	5:00 Pace	6:00 Pace
Start	09:15	10:00	10:00	10:00	10:00	14	10:29	11:52	12:24	12:40	13:12
1	09:20	10:08	10:10	10:11	10:14	15	10:35	12:00	12:34	12:51	13:26
2	09:25	10:16	10:20	10:22	10:27	16	10:40	12:08	12:44	13:03	13:40
3	09:31	10:24	10:30	10:34	10:41	17	10:45	12:16	12:55	13:14	13:54
4	09:36	10:32	10:41	10:45	10:55	18	10:51	12:24	13:05	13:26	14:07
5	09:41	10:40	10:51	10:57	11:09	19	10:56	12:32	13:15	13:37	14:21
6	09:47	10:48	11:01	11:08	11:22	20	11:01	12:40	13:26	13:49	14:35
7	09:52	10:56	11:12	11:20	11:36	21	11:07	12:48	13:36	14:00	14:49
8	09:57	11:04	11:22	11:31	11:50	22	11:12	12:56	13:46	14:11	15:02
9	10:03	11:12	11:32	11:43	12:04	23	11:17	13:04	13:56	14:23	15:16
10	10:08	11:20	11:43	11:54	12:18	24	11:23	13:12	14:07	14:34	15:30
11	10:13	11:28	11:53	12:05	12:31	25	11:28	13:20	14:17	14:46	15:44
12	10:19	11:36	12:03	12:17	12:45	26	11:33	13:28	14:27	14:57	15:57
13	10:24	11:44	12:13	12:28	12:59	Finish	11:35	13:30	14:30	14:00	16:00

1) How much earlier did the Elite Women pass the 18 mile marker?

2) Using the information given for 18 miles, find out the average time taken for the Elite Women to run each mile. Round your answer to the **nearest hundredth of a minute**.

3) Gammon reaches the 18 mile marker $57\frac{1}{2}$ minutes later than Hailey. If he continues at the same pace, how many more minutes does he have to run?

DV FILES

Gammon decides to draw some tessellations of his own.

He notices that some are not true tessellations because there are gaps between the shapes when they are placed side to side.

1) Investigate to find out which **regular** shapes do tessellate and why.

2) Calculate the angles of the shape formed by the gap between these regular pentagons.

3) Now calculate the angles of other 'gap' shapes formed by trying to tessellate octagons or nonagons.

Now I'm so far behind, I think I'll take some photographs inside St Paul's Cathedral! Wooo hooo, look at all the patterns!

Huxley's Helpline

Use what you know about properties of 2-D shapes to help calculate angles.

TIME: *Rush hour*
PLACE: *Stuck in a right old jam*

Huxley and co. have been given the task of finding a solution to the nation's traffic jam problems due to the sabotage of all the traffic light systems across the country. Someone has pinched all the coloured lights.

Well, we've been given the green light for this mission.

It's the green lights we need to be fixing!

TM

At *Academy Junction*, just outside the Brain Academy headquarters, the green light is on for 22 seconds. The amber light is then on for $\frac{1}{20}$ of a minute. The traffic coming from the other direction must then wait for $\frac{1}{30}$ minute on red and amber before their light goes green.

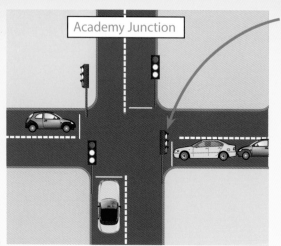

Academy Junction

The light has just turned green.

1) How many seconds must the white car wait for another green light?

2) On average, 18 cars pass through one green light. There are another 56 cars in a queue behind this yellow one. How long will it take for all these cars to go across *Academy Junction*?

MM

The team look at the CCTV camera footage from around the country. Strangely, the same white and blue vans keep appearing in the dead of night! They can just make out some of the registration numbers.

1) What pattern has Huxley spotted?

2) What does the registration number look like on plate D?

Look, I've spotted a pattern. The numbers decrease by the same amount each time!

a **MCM LXVI**

b **MDC LVII**

c **MCCC XLVIII**

d **?**

DV FILES

The police car is the red dot. ● Find the new coordinates when:

1) The police car moves so it is exactly halfway between vans **A** and **D**.

2) Van **C** moves to make a parallelogram with the other vans **A**, **B** and **D**.

3) Van **B** translates to $(x + 1, y - 5)$.

4) The **car is at the** centre point of a circle with diameter from van **A** to the **new position** of van **C**.

Soon other police cars are called for back-up and they have the thieves surrounded. It's off to prison for them, but not before they have replaced all the stolen traffic lights!

The team call WPC Gallop and PC Trott, who will pass on the details to Scotland Yard.

They will find the thieves now!

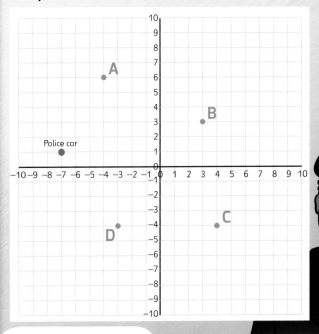

What did the traffic light say to the car?

Don't look, I'm changing!

Huxley's Helpline

You may find it easier to turn the book around to help find the parallelogram.

TIME: *To get your 'five a day'*
PLACE: *Fiasco's Supermarket*

Rosa is charting the distribution of the new hybrid vegetables: the Carrocado, Broccopea and Pumptato that have taken the country by storm and are in demand in every shop and supermarket.

So Rosa, the idea of mixing the genetic codes of different vegetables to create new types of vegetable is certainly 'growing on me'.

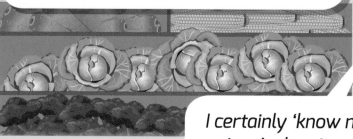

I certainly 'know my onions' when it comes to growing stuff, Sir!

TM

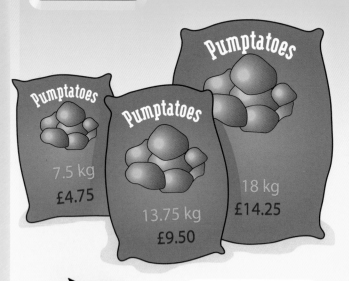

Pumptatoes
7.5 kg
£4.75

Pumptatoes
13.75 kg
£9.50

Pumptatoes
18 kg
£14.25

1) The Fiasco Supermarket places an order for 178 kg of pumptatoes. Rosa sends them 12 sacks of Pumptatoes. How many of each sack did she send them?

2) How much did the order cost? Could the same mass of Pumptatoes in a different number of bags have cost less? Explain your thinking.

3) Why does Omar think Rosa has made a mistake? Prove your thinking showing calculations you have used.

4) What is the most Rosa should charge for the 13.75 kg bag and the 18 kg bag? Why?

Rosa, I don't think your pricing is right.

Rosa has charted the mass of each vegetable sold over the past months. She is thrilled with the results!

1) What is the difference between the total mass sold in April and August?

2) Approximately what mass of Carrocados was sold on the 10th June?

3) Which vegetable was the best seller over these past months?
How do you know?

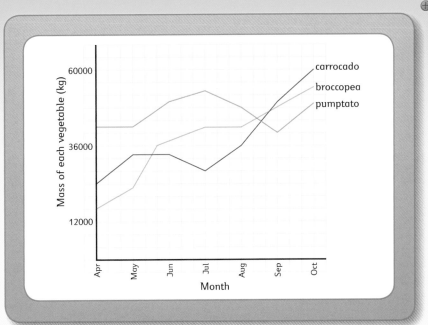

DV FILES

Rosa would like to make a pie chart to show the proportion of each vegetable sold in July.

She would like to compare it to those sold in October.

1) Draw a pie chart for July and another for October.

2) Compare the proportions of each vegetable sold showing any differences as a percentage.

What do you get if you cross Brussels sprouts with baked beans?

Enough gas to power the country I believe. What a great idea!

Huxley's Helpline

Round decimals to the nearest hundredth.

TIME: To get the builders in
PLACE: Home sweet home

Mason has designed an extension to the Brain Academy base. It is designed to blend in with the environment through camouflage and is almost invisible.

Right, you said you were building an extension, Mason. Well, where is it?

Err, right in front of your digital live-cam eye, Sir!

TM

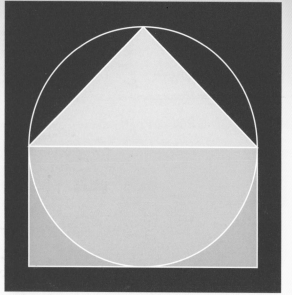

Here is the plan of Mason's rather wacky design. The diameter of the circle on the plan is 9.8 cm. Use this information to:

1) Find the dimensions of the rectangle.

2) Find the area of the triangle.

3) Find the **actual area** of the rectangle if the diameter of the circle in the actual extension is **24.5 metres**.

4) What scale has Mason used for his plan?

Here is one of the walls to be painted. Mason must calculate how much paint he needs.

6 m

24.5 m

1) Use the information you have to complete the table.

2) Paint comes in tins of 5 litres or 2.5 litres. How many of each should he buy so he can paint three walls of this size?

3) How much paint will he have left over? _____ **litres**. What fraction of the tin is this?

Surface area	
Spreading rate of paint per litre	12 m²
Number of coats of paint	3
Total paint required	

DV FILES

Mason is keen to camouflage the extension so it becomes almost invisible.

He begins to mix different paints just to get the right colours for all three walls.

He first mixes **28.5** litres of each of these.

1) How many litres of green paint has he used in total?

2) How about yellow and black?

3) For the remaining paint, he uses 19.8 litres of green paint to mix with yellow. What ratio does Mason use this time?

He uses the following ratios of different colour paints

green: yellow
3 : 2

black : green
7 : 9

black : yellow
5 : 7

Huxley's Helpline

For question 3, remember that you already know how much paint Mason needs in total from the **Main Mission**.

TIME: The end is nigh
PLACE: Space Rock Earth

Most extinctions have occurred naturally, before humans walked on Earth. It is estimated that 99.9% of all species that have ever existed are now extinct. The team has been asked by the Worldwide Fund for Nature to help find out more.

I don't like the idea of species becoming extinct.

No, but it has happened since life began on this planet, Sir. Heavy thoughts!

TM

The total number of known extinct species is 905. Most extinctions happened in the last century. Remember that a species is a group of animals, plants or living things that share common characteristics.

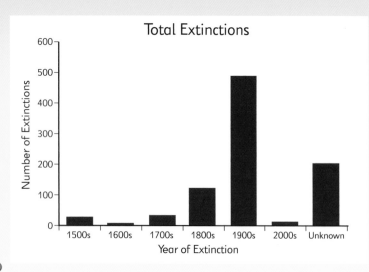

Total Extinctions

1) Approximately how many species became extinct in each century?

2) Approximately what percentage of the total 905 species became extinct at an unknown time? Round your answer to the nearest **tenth**.

3) What is the ratio of extinctions in the 1800s to the 2000s? Give your answer in its **lowest** form.

MM

Babs uses her computer to find out more about endangered species in 2014. There are 41,415 species on the Red List of Threatened Species with 16,306 threatened with extinction. Here are some of the mammals.

	Population in 2014	Height (Maximum)	Mass (maximum)	Reasons for being critically endangered
Black Rhino	4848	1.57 m	1397 kg	Poaching Destruction of habitat
Mountain Gorilla	880	1.65 m when standing	199.6 kg	Harmed by poaching of other animals Destruction of habitat
Sumatran Elephant	2400–2800	2.74 m (at shoulders)	5000 kg	Poaching Destruction of habitat Elephant/human conflict
Sumatran Tiger	< 400	1.1 m (at shoulders)	139.7 kg	Poaching Destruction of habitat

1) What is the mean maximum mass of the four mammals?

2) In 1970 the population of black rhino was 60,000. Approximately how many times smaller is the population in 2014? White your answer to the nearest **thousandth**.

3) What fraction of the height of the mountain gorilla is the Sumatran tiger? Write the fraction in its simplest form.

DV FILES

Rosa, Evan and Mason go out to help the Elephant Flying Squad in central Sumatra.

The Squad is made up of rangers, noise and light-making devices, a truck, and four trained elephants that drive the wild elephants away from local villages.

1) Convert each of the lengths here to metres.

2) What is the area of the village in square metres?

3) The light-making devices should be placed at a maximum of 85 feet from each other. There must always be one at a corner. What is the minimum number needed to protect the red part of the perimeter?

This is the plan of one village.

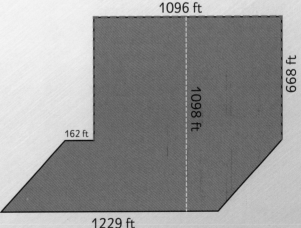

1096 ft

668 ft

1098 ft

162 ft

1229 ft

Huxley's Helpline

Use the conversion 1 foot ≈ 30 cm.

TIME: To fetch your nets
PLACE: Deep trouble!

Omar has rescued some rare species of fish, of different sizes, from an environmental disaster: a spillage of coloured paints into the local park's lake. The fish need to be cared for in special tanks.

Our fishy friends are painting a pretty picture.

They're looking like their tropical cousins: multi-coloured.

TM

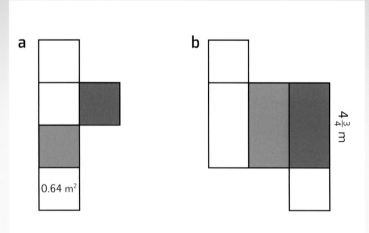

a

0.64 m²

b

$4\frac{3}{4}$ m

Omar has designed these nets for the fish tanks.

1) Is the orange or blue face better for the base of each tank?

2) What is the volume of Tank A? _____ m³ or _____ cm³

3) The shorter side of the base in Tank B is half the length of the longer side. What is the area of the base? Give your answer as a mixed number of square metres.

MM

Omar records the number of fish in each tank using a multiplication calculation. He only writes whole numbers less than 10 and uses the X sign and the **square** and **cube** symbols.

1) What calculation could Omar write for each tank?

2) Why can Omar not write a calculation like this to show the total of all three tanks?

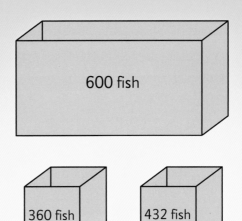

600 fish

360 fish

432 fish

DV FILES

Based on the shape of the fish scales, Huxley decides to make up a puzzle with a net of a tetrahedron for Omar to solve.

Place each number in the net so that the white triangles are always the **sum** of the **three** coloured triangles around it. Where **two** different coloured triangles touch, the numbers have a difference of 0.4.

$1\frac{19}{20}$

$\frac{23}{10}$

$3\frac{47}{60}$

$\frac{13}{30}$

1.2

$1\frac{3}{5}$ $1\frac{7}{30}$ 0.375

$\frac{10}{5}$

$\frac{5}{6}$ $4\frac{1}{8}$ $1\frac{7}{20}$ $\frac{4}{15}$

1.75

$\frac{9}{20}$

$\frac{2}{3}$

Glad to see the pond life back to normal.

Indeed, no need to carp on about it now Omar!

Huxley's Helpline

Remember to think about fraction and decimal equivalents

29

5.12 B.A. Rollercoaster Festival

TIME: To get the sick bags ready
PLACE: The best theme park ever

Mason has designed a whole new theme park with thrilling rides. Rollercoasters, log-flumes, virtual reality rides, restaurants and shops are all top notch.

Can I have a go on the rides, Mason?

TM

Of course, Sir! Just don't leave any charging plugs and wires dangling over the side.

The virtual reality rides take passengers into space. They will see the different planets up close and personal and can even experience walking on the Moon!

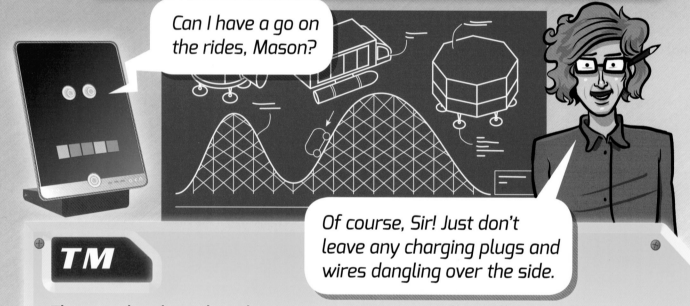

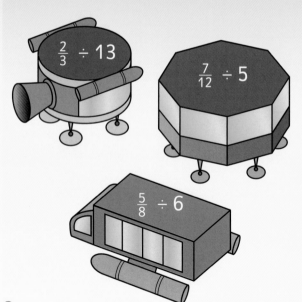

$\frac{2}{3} \div 13$

$\frac{7}{12} \div 5$

$\frac{5}{8} \div 6$

There are **three** space cars on the shuttle. Each of the space cars has a number of VIP seats ready for the grand opening.

1) Find the fraction of VIP seats in each car using the division calculations.

2) There are a total of 147 seats available on the shuttle. Using what you know from question 1, find the total number of seats that are available on the shuttle for other passengers.

3) What fraction is this of the total number of seats on the shuttle?

It is time for the grand opening ceremony. All the Brain Academy team have come to support Mason. The visitors flock to the different rides.
The different attractions took a total of £9679 during the morning. Money was taken at each ride and includes balloons and candyfloss bought at the time.

1) Complete the table.

2) The restaurants took a total of £5480 that morning. What percentage of the total park takings does the Log-Flume represent now?

Attraction	Fraction of total	Amount taken
Log-Flume	11.5%	
Shooting Space Shuttle	0.24	
Rollercoaster	$\frac{3}{8}$	
Crazy Carousel	Mean of 3 rides above	
Mirror Maze		Remaining amount

DV FILES

Mason wants to chart the height of the Rollercoaster every 5 seconds of the ride.

1) Use the line graph to help complete the table below.

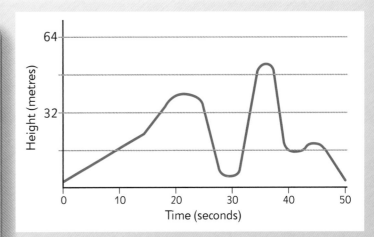

Time (secs)	0	5									50
Height (m)											

2) For approximately how many seconds in total is the Rollercoaster ≥ 32 m high?

Huxley's Helpline

You may find it useful to use a ruler to help make decisions about some of the heights.

5.13 B.A.R.F. Alert!

TIME: To fix it!
PLACE: The ex-best theme park ever ...

All the rides and attractions start to go wrong leaving the visitors stranded in mid-ride. Huxley and the team have to perform a rescue. After a spectacular morning, Mason was not expecting things to go so terribly wrong...

Good job nobody's been hurt. Yet ...

Life is a rollercoaster sometimes, Hux old chap.

TM

Babs, Omar and Evan race to the Big Wheel. They notice that the cars are numbered in rather a strange way.

1) Starting with 101 and going in a clockwise direction, find the rule and the missing numbers in this linear sequence.

2) Evan sets up an ingenious contraption of pulleys and chains that rotates the wheel through exactly 67.5° to a stop position. After how many of these turns will the passengers in **car 101** be rescued?

Huxley, Hailey and Gammon make their way up the emergency steps to the top of the log flume. The log car is **balanced** right at the very top!

The total mass of the 11 passengers is shown here. **No passengers weigh the same.** Only **two** passengers weigh a **whole number** of kg. **No passenger weighs less** than **55 kg**.

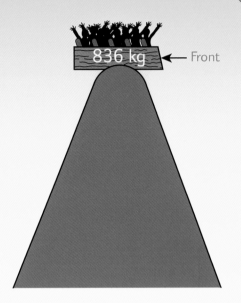

836 kg ← Front

1) Find a possible set of weights for the 11 passengers.

2) If the passenger in the middle of the log car weighs $\frac{5}{44}$ of the total mass, what does that tell you about the mass of the front four passengers?

3) Hailey rescues **two** passengers from the rear of the log car with a combined mass of 183 kg. Gammon rescues three passengers from the front. The log car is still balanced. Find a possible set of weights for all 11 passengers now.

DV FILES

In the Whirling Water Pipe, Rosa and Mason must lower the water level so that the Toppling Tub returns to the base of an empty pipe.

The current water level is $\frac{5}{24}$ from the top. 1280 litres of water can be released at a time. Rosa and Mason let **more than** 58 lots of 1280 litres out. They only have to use 97.5% of the last lot of water.

1) Investigate to find out the possible number of litres of water released.

2) **The Pipe holds a whole number of litres when full.** Find the minimum number of litres of water the Pipe could hold?

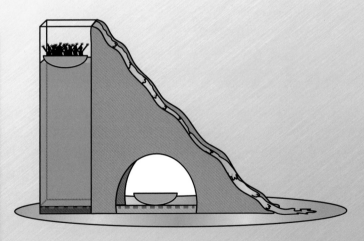

Hmm ... 'thrills and spills'. Best not to have the spills ...

Huxley's Helpline

Round any decimals to the nearest thousandth of a litre.

TIME: To be brave
PLACE: On the edge ...

The Brain Academy team is going bungee jumping to raise money for the charity C.H.U.F. (Children Having Unbelievable Fun).

Well done everyone for taking part, very brave indeed.

Err, I think you need to lead by example, Sir!

TM

height of jump

Evan explains that on a bungee jump, the cord will only stretch to four times its length to make it safe. To calculate the length of the cord before a jump, they simply find $\frac{1}{4}$ of the height of the jump. They then change the thickness of the cord for people of different weights.

1) The height of this jump is between 150 and 200 feet. Suggest **five** possible heights of this jump and the length of the rubber cord each time. Put your answers in a table with these headings.

Height of jump in feet	Height of jump in metres	Length of cord in metres

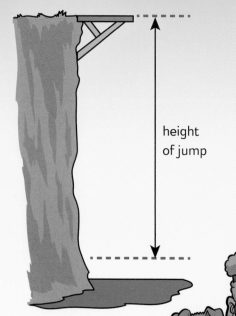

Remember that there are 12 inches in 1 foot. 1 inch ≈ 2.5 cm

Some of the team are still rather nervous and want to know a bit more about the rubber bungee cord. Rosa and Omar decide they want to test this out for themselves.

	Original cord length	Stretched length at breaking point
A	19 cm	cm
B	cm	1206 cm
C	1.2 m	m
D	0.7 m	m
E	2.5 m	m

1) Use the information to complete the table.

2) Rosa tests another rubber cord. It breaks at exactly 2000 mm. What was the original length? Round your answer to the nearest **whole millimetre**.

Research shows that a strand of rubber cord will break at 6.7 times its length when stretched out.

DV FILES

The bungee jumps are about to begin. If all goes to plan, the team will reach the target amount of money for the charity C.H.U.F.

Each team member will raise a different amount of money. The amount a team member raises is always 2% more of the total target of £125,000 than the person below them in the list, e.g. Gammon raises 2% more of the target than Mason.

1) Find out what percentage of the total amount each team member will raise.

2) Now find how much money they each raise for C.H.U.F.

1	Evan
2	Hailey
3	Omar
4	Huxley
5	Babs
6	Rosa
7	Gammon
8	Mason

TARGET

£125,000

There's no way I could've jumped – I'm wireless and made of glass.

Of course, Sir, plus you don't have legs to attach the rope to!

Huxley's Helpline

You may find it helpful to start with Mason.

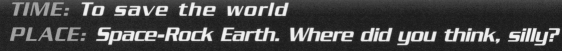

TIME: To save the world
PLACE: Space-Rock Earth. Where did you think, silly?

The team has been asked to combat a mad villain, Doctor Soft!
Doc Soft has built a giant laser satellite and he is threatening to
destroy the trees and rainforests around the world!
No trees? No oxygen!

> Who will help us rid of the World of Soft? That spongy scientist will have us all gasping for breath. Well not me, obviously *coughs, digitally*.

> He doesn't sound very dangerous with a name like that, Sir: 'Soft'? Are you sure?

TM

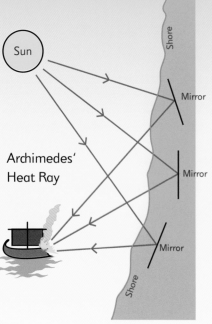

Sun

Archimedes' Heat Ray

Shore

Mirror

Mirror

Mirror

Shore

Archimedes is one of the greatest mathematicians of all time. You may have heard of the Greek word 'Eureka!' He shouted this as he ran into the street because he had found a way to calculate the volume of an object with an irregular shape. This was a gold crown.

Archimedes was also famous for burning enemy Roman warships by setting up rows of mirrors. This was called the 'Heat Ray'.

1) Measure each of the angles made as the Sun's rays hit and bounce off the mirrors.

2) Draw your own sketch of a ray bouncing off a mirror at 78°.

3) Wood ignites at a temperature of 570 degrees Fahrenheit (°F). What is this temperature in degrees Celsius (°C)? Use this equation to help you:

$$(°C \times 1.8) + 32 = °F$$

There have been sightings of the laser satellite from three major cities. Some forests have already been scorched. The team must 'Stop Soft' before it's too late!

I have an idea. Let's ask NASA to change the direction of the Earth's satellite 'Spudstar' so that its signal scrambles the one being sent to the laser!

Asuncion	Tue 12:56	Dubai	Tue 20:56	London*	Tue 17:56	São Paulo	Tue 13:56
Athens*	Tue 19:56	Dublin*	Tue 17:56	Los Angeles*	Tue 09:56	Seattle*	Tue 09:56
Atlanta*	Tue 12:56	Edmonton*	Tue 10:56	Madrid*	Tue 18:56	Seoul	Tue 01:56

* = adjusted for daylight saving time (DST) or summer time

NASA reports that there will be a **478 second delay** before *Spudstar* begins to change direction.

1) What time will it be in London, Dubai and Atlanta when this happens?

2) How much later will it be in Seoul than Los Angeles?

3) It is no longer Tuesday in Hanoi (not shown here). Why?

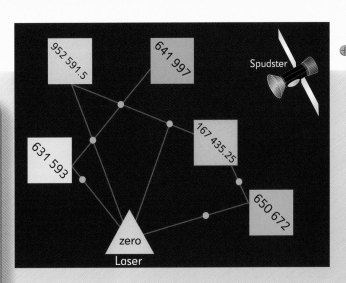

DV FILES

Spudstar starts to move and its signals fill the airwaves above Earth.

The lasers from Doctor Soft's laser satellite become confused and rays are beaming in all different directions!

Spudstar must aim its signals at each of the yellow dots to scramble Doc Soft's laser rays. Each yellow dot is positioned a fraction of the way between the numbers in a pair of squares.

1) Help the BA team save the trees by finding the value of each yellow dot to instruct Spudstar where to aim.

Doc Soft has been sorted, for now. But I doubt we've heard the last of that mad, mash-able, meddling medic!

Huxley's Helpline

For example, if a yellow dot is placed halfway between 1000 and 1250, *Spudstar* would need to aim at 1125.

5.16 Loch Ness? Oh Yes!

TIME: 8 'o'Loch' in the morning
PLACE: On the banks of Loch Ness in Bonnie Scotland

Babs is working on her wooden computer with data collected from the Brain Academy 'mini-sub' (piloted by Gammon) that is exploring the bottom of Loch Ness. There can't really be a monster lurking in the depths, can there?

I saw something with a long neck, slimy skin and big beady AiAi-eyes!

You can't have done: Huxley's on holiday!

TM

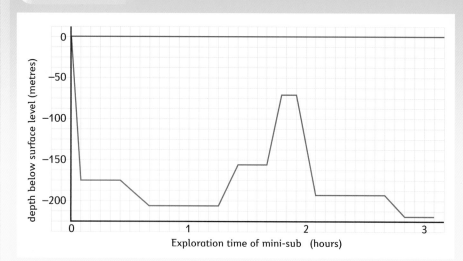

Exploration time of mini-sub (hours)

depth below surface level (metres)

1) Help complete Babs' table for the total journey shown above.

Great, I can now see the exact path that Gammon took and complete my table!

Time (minutes)	0	20	40	60	
Depth (metres)	0				

Gammon started exploring Loch Ness at **14:36**. He soared towards the surface and took a photograph of something rather mysterious … could it be a monster?

1) At what time do you think he took the photograph of this 'monster'? How do you know?

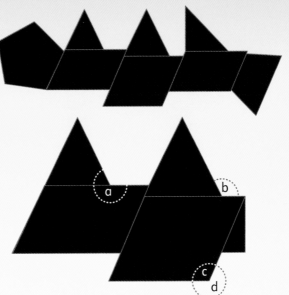

2) Babs can see some 2-D shapes and lots of angles in the photograph. Without using a protractor, find the size of each of the angles **a**, **b**, **c** and **d**. Explain any decisions you have made.

DV FILES

Babs looks at another of the photographs that Gammon has taken of a 'monster'.

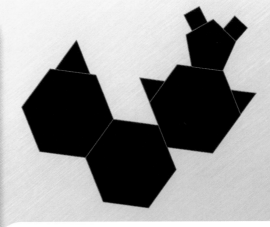

She calculates that the perimeter of a single hexagon is 14.4 cm.

1) Find the perimeter of the whole 'monster' shape.

2) The final photograph shows the same nine shapes, but this time, the perimeter of the 'monster' shape is **37 cm**. Sketch and label the possible shape of the monster in the last photograph.

How do you make contact with a creature down so deep in the Loch?

We could always drop it a line. HeHeHe!

Huxley's Helpline

Use what you know about properties of 2-D shapes to help you.

TIME: *To get your clubs out*
PLACE: *Seaside towns around the country*

Evan is the Brain Academy Crazy Golf Champion. He's been trying to reinvigorate the seaside holiday trade by popularizing the game.

> *Well the queues for our local course are longer than usual. What have you done, Evan?*

> *Free Crazy Golf, Sir. Once everyone discovers how much fun it is, they'll come and pay.*

TM

½ m

3¾ m

3⅕ m

⅞ m

This is Evan's favourite hole. The golf ball must go through the mouth of the dragon so it comes out in the rear part of the green.

1) Ignoring the dragon's head, what is the area of the front part of the green? Give your answer as a **mixed number**.

2) How much smaller is the rear part?

3) Evan's ball went into the hole after **three** putts, but poor Gammon took **eight** putts. What proportion of the putts was taken by Evan?

Rosa and Huxley prefer the windmill hole. It is always rather a challenge getting the ball through the right exit under the windmill. The table below shows the number of putts each team member took to complete the hole.

	Rosa	Huxley	Omar	Babs
Number of putts	4	3		9
	Evan	Gammon	Mason	Hailey
Number of putts		7	6	

1) If the mean number of putts for the second four players was **5.75**, find some possible number of putts for Evan and Hailey.

2) If the mean number of putts for all players was **5.875**, how many putts did Omar take?

DV FILES

The Brain Academy team have been helping to make Crazy Golf popular again so much so that Da Vinci has reported queues at every course around the country. It's still free though!

1) Complete the rest of Da Vinci's report.

2) What percentage of the total number of people were queueing at Sandy Shallows?

Course	Da Vinci's report	Total number of people in queues over 18 days
Little Boulders	$3^3 \times 4^2 \times 17$	
Black Puddle	$\_^3 \times 5^2 \times 6$	9600
Small Pebbles	$5^3 \times \_\_^2 \times 2^2$	4-digit cube number larger than 3200
Sandy Shallows	$6^3 \times (5^2 + 17)$	
Shady Shingles	$7^3 + (\_\_ \times 9^2)$	1396

Hmm. Perhaps 50p a game might work.

Huxley's Helpline

Round your percentage to the nearest tenth of a percent.

MISSION 5.18 Oh My Frog!

TIME: *To hop it (sorry)*
PLACE: *In the 'croakroom' (sorry again)*

Omar has collected samples of Amazonian frogs, some of which are very poisonous, and placed them in safe containers to study. However, he's dropped the tray and some of the frogs have escaped. Their poisons are precious: they could be used for a medical breakthrough.

These froggy friends will prove useful. Just don't lick them, Omar ...

No time to lick one, Sir, I've got to catch them before anything else!

TM

Omar had placed some of the poisonous frogs in three different trays.

1) Use the algebraic statements below to find the number of frogs in each tray.

$$a + 12c = b^2 \qquad 6^3 - c = 168 \qquad \frac{3c}{2^3} = 43 - b$$

2) Omar had another 78 frogs in a larger tray. What percentage of his total frog collection was in **Tray b**?

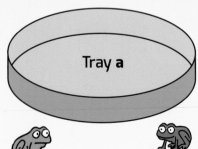

Tray **a**

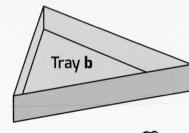

Tray **b**

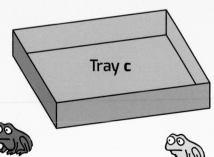

Tray **c**

Omar investigates some different amounts of poison and other ingredients to make a serum.

Omar's Fantastic Frog Serum

Plant extract	14.5 % of serum
Sugar solution	?
Frog poison	126.7 ml
Mystery liquid	$\frac{7}{18}$ of serum

Frog poison   <   Sugar solution   <   Mystery liquid
Total serum is a multiple of 0.03 litres

1) Find at least five different ways to make this true.

2) What is the least amount of serum that Omar can make? Give your answer in **ml**.

3) Is there a maximum amount of sugar solution that can be used in the serum?

DV FILES

Before long the number of frogs has multiplied and Omar must separate them into different trays.

Place a **three-digit** number of frogs in each of the **triangular trays** so that:

- The **product** of a pair of triangular trays on a line is a **multiple of 17**.

- The number of frogs in each rectangular tray is a **prime** number but is also the **difference** between the two triangular trays on either side of it.

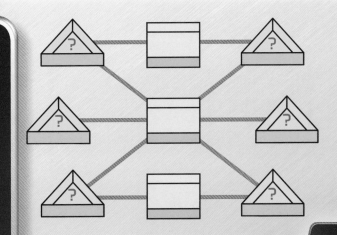

We're lucky; this is a good time for frog breeding, Omar.

Is it a leap year, Sir?

Huxley's Helpline

Think about whether it is possible for all the prime numbers to be different.

Problem-solving Strategies

Use the TASC Problem Solving Wheel to help you. TASC means Thinking Actively in a Social Context.

Learn from experience

Communicate

Reflect
What have I learned?

What have I learned?

Let's tell someone.

Communicate
Who can I tell?

TA

How well did I do?

Evaluate

Evaluate
Did I succeed? Can I think of another way?

Let's do it!

Implement
Now let me do it!

Implement

We can learn to be expert thinkers!

Gather/organise

What do I know about this?

Gather/organise
What do I know about this?

What is the task?

Identify
What is the task?

Identify

How many ideas can I think of?

Generate
How many ideas can I think of?

Generate

Which is the best idea?

Decide

Decide
Which is the best idea?

S C

Mission Strategies

Mission 5.1

Carefully trace the diagram in the Da Vinci Files or ask your teacher to make a copy of it so you can clearly show the size of each angle. Remember, no protractors allowed in this one!

Mission 5.2

You may find it useful to cut out a hotel template and move it on the grid to check your decisions in the Main Mission.

Mission 5.3

Remember to check both scales on the time graph in the Main Mission. Think about the values that are between the written labels. This is a tricky one because you have two sets of information to think about …

Mission 5.4

Don't forget that it is easier to complete addition and subtraction calculations with fractions when they share the same denominator.

Mission 5.5

When working on algebraic logic problems like in the Main Mission, remember to read all clues first so you can decide which one will be the most useful starting place.

Mission 5.6

In the Training Mission, you could draw a table or make a list to help you keep track of the distance that Gammon runs compared to Hailey. Remember that you need to find out the point when Hailey reaches exactly 16 miles.

Mission 5.7

Remember that the traffic is queueing in two directions at Academy Junction. Each set of cars must wait for the sequence in the other direction to finish before their own sequence starts again.

Mission 5.8

Use a table or make a list of your calculations in the Training Mission. This will help you work towards a solution for question 1 by trying out different possibilities and adjusting them as you go along. Remember that Rosa sends 12 sacks!

Mission 5.9

When you are calculating, always remember to think about a mental method first. Then consider a written method or decide to use a calculator if the calculation is too tricky or you need to try lots of different ideas without losing track of your thinking.

Mission 5.10

If you are not sure how to find the area of the village in the Da Vinci Files, you could carefully trace the shape and then cut it up into useful pieces to help you.

Mission 5.11

If you find it difficult to visualise the nets in the Training Mission, you can draw or trace a template to fold. This will help you to make decisions.

Mission 5.12

Remember to check both scales on the line graph and think about the values that are between the written labels. Fractions will help you with all of the missions here.

Mission 5.13

Work with a partner or in a small group to help you solve the Da Vinci Files. You will need to try out different ideas and reason about possible amounts of water. Talking about mathematical problems with others is a big help.

Mission 5.14

Remember that you need to convert feet to metres in the Training Mission. Try to think about how you can use mental methods for this and when finding a quarter.

Mission 5.15

In the Main Mission, not all the information you need is shown in the table so you will need to think about a possible answer and explain your decision. Try explaining your decision to a friend first.

Mission 5.16

Work with a partner or in a small group to help you solve the Da Vinci Files. Each person could be in charge of investigating the dimensions of one of the shapes and reporting back to the group.

Mission 5.17

Use what you know about 2-D shapes to help find any missing lengths on the green areas in the Training Mission.

Mission 5.18

In the Da Vinci Files, you may find it useful to write each possible number on separate pieces of paper and then move them around the grid as you check for a solution.

National Association for Able Children in Education

What is NACE?

NACE, a registered charity founded in 1983, is the leading independent organisation for the education of the more able.

What does NACE do?

NACE specialises in working with teachers and schools to improve learning for the more able and to turn ability into achievement for all.

The NACE community provides teachers with:
A members' website including:
- Guidance and resources
- New to A,G&T
- Subject specific resources
- Specialist advice
- An award winning monthly E-bulletin packed with sources of inspiration and regular updates
- NACE Insight, a termly newsletter

How will the book help me?

The *Brain Academy* Maths Mission Files challenge and help you to become better at learning and a better mathematician by:
- thinking of and testing different solutions to problems
- making connections to what you already know
- working by yourself and with others
- expecting you to get better and to go on to the next book
- learning skills which you can use in other subjects and out of school.

We hope you enjoy the books!